# Ross's

# Communicative Discoveries

## Michael Ross

# Ross's

# Communicative
# Discoveries

## Michael Ross

Rare Bird • Los Angeles, Calif.

THIS IS A GENUINE RARE BIRD BOOK

A Rare Bird Book | Rare Bird Books
453 South Spring Street, Suite 302
Los Angeles, CA 90013
rarebirdbooks.com

Set in Minion
Printed in the United States
Distributed worldwide by Publishers Group West

Publisher's Cataloging-in-Publication Data
Names: Ross, Michael, author.
Title: Ross's Communicative Discoveries: Quotes from Literary Fiction
on Personal Communications / Michael Ross.
Series: Ross's Quotations.
Description: First Hardcover Edition | A Genuine Rare Bird Book | New York, NY;
Los Angeles, CA: Rare Bird Books, 2019.
Identifiers: ISBN 9781644280843
Subjects: LCSH Communication—Quotations, maxims, etc. | Quotations, English. |
BISAC REFERENCE / Quotations
Classification: LCC PN90 .R67 2019 | DDC 302.2—dc23

*To my family, friends, classmates,*
*shipmates, colleagues, students,*
*and other men and women*
*—you know who you are.*

# Introduction

One of the tasks that becomes more difficult for each successive volume of my collection of quotations is writing the introduction. On the one hand, I do not want to repeat too much of what I have written in *Ross's Novel Discoveries, Ross's Timely Discoveries, Ross's Thoughtful Discoveries,* and *Ross's Personal Discoveries*. On the other hand, it seems like it would be shameless promotion of those volumes for me simply to refer readers of this volume who do not have, or have not read, them to the introductions to those books.

In each prior volume, I described my experience reading literary fiction over the years, at least since graduating as an English major in college. I have read more than 1,350 books, of which most are works by a wide variety of authors classic, modern and contemporary novels, short stories and plays. I noted some of the changes in my reading habits over the years, especially since the publication of my earlier books. One effect has been my effort to broaden my selection of authors, not so much to find more or better quotations but rather to discover more excellent literary fiction. Looking back, I found that my selection was principally male US authors, so I have sampled more foreign and female authors. I have also increased my efforts to read novels set in locations where we are traveling, such as, Paul Bowles in Morocco, Carlos Ruiz Zafon in Barcelona, Eleanor Catton in New Zealand and César Aira in South America. A result is that I have a larger collection of books waiting to be read. I am still inclined to read additional works by authors whose books I have enjoyed.

Another effect, which I try to constrain, is to consider to some extent which authors and books might contribute good quotes for my collection. Although some authors have contributed more than their fair share, such as, Gore Vidal, José

Saramago and Carlos Fuentes in this volume, there are many excellent writers whose works I enjoy but which have contributed few quotes, such as, those by Mario Vargas Llosa and Kazuo Ishiguro. I try not to let my desire to share quotes diminish the quality of literary fiction I read. I have also been putting more books aside unfinished after I have given them a fair opportunity to make a favorable impression. These include works by authors whose works I have previously admired.

I also offered explanations of my association with the topics covered in each volume. My choice for quotes about communications for this book was motivated, in part, because the subject seems to follow naturally after the quotes in *Ross's Personal Discoveries* on personal relations, which are, naturally, heavily dependent upon communications between or among the people in various relationships. The positive, negative or changing nature of our relations is affected, intentionally or not, by our dialogues, monologues, conversations, debates and discussions.

At my age, I have had a quite a few personal relations with, for example, my parents, brother and sister and their families, our son and daughter, friends, fraternity brothers, colleagues and lovers. It would be false to claim that I have been uniformly successful in my efforts to communicate my thoughts and feelings to all or any of these audiences. My failures have contributed to failed relationships, but I hope some of my successes have helped create and maintain positive relations. In each case, I know I have learned some valuable lessons. I also try to learn from my reading of literary fiction. I am reminded of a few quotes from prior volumes: "Women, unlike men, actually notice things," from Richard Russo's *Bridge of Sighs*. "Isn't it funny how paradise always lies in the past or the future, never exactly in the present?" from John Updike's *S*; and "The only thing I know for sure is you can never be too misinformed," from Richard Powers' *Generosity, an Enhancement*.

My varied professional endeavors have also offered me some insight into the pitfalls with communications. During my tours of duty in the Navy, I responded to commands from senior officers, reacted to requests, suggestions and complaints by junior officers and enlisted men. I also learned how to ghost-write the captains' responses to their superiors. It was valuable at a relatively young age to learn the importance of concise, accurate communications, upon which the fleet underway depends. In my law firm practice, I learned communication skills and foibles from mentors and other senior partners, my peers, members of the mergers and acquisition teams I led and negotiators on the other side of deals. I was not surprised to find that I learned a great deal about communications while I was teaching students in the US and abroad.

Over time, through these varied experiences, I learned the value of listening, which may be one of the most important lessons. I gained an appreciation for the benefits of silence. I learned the value of timely concessions and the importance of concise communications both orally and in writing. Although this book is not directed to professional communications, I think that some of the quotes may be relevant in the professional world.

# Difficulties and Complications

Many narrators and characters comment on how difficult and complicated communications among us can be. Some of the reasons appear to be inadequacies of our means of communication, that is, our words themselves. As many of us have learned through our ineffective efforts to communicate our thoughts, words were not enough or did not serve us well. All of this seems a bit ironic coming from authors who, by definition, ply their trade with words.

The first quote in this section claims that
we do not have access to sufficient means
to communicate what we want.

«»

*Human vocabulary is still not capable,
and probably never will be, of knowing,
recognizing, and communicating everything
that can be humanly experienced and felt.*

José Saramago, The Cave

What we have are words, and, if they have
a life of their own, they may try their best
to serve us well.

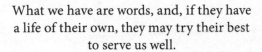

*...a cluster of syllables tries to form a word
and the word...painstakingly seeks its
related words (friendly or enemy words) to
form an image.*

Carlos Fuentes, "La Desdichada"
in *Constancia and Other
Stories for Virgins*

Try as we and words might, the ones we have at our disposal may not be true to some objective standard of truth.

«»

*Words, as is well known, are the great foes of reality.*

Joseph Conrad, *Under Western Eyes*

Here is a strongly worded expression of dismay that words can mean more, less or something different than what we intend.

«»

*It was a sinister thing to discover at such an age, that words can escape their meanings.*

Don Delillo, *End Zone*

This is a simple warning, but without any
guidance for what to do about
the problem.

«»

*Words can give wrong ideas.*

V. S. Naipaul, *Magic Seeds*

The college teacher in this novel offers
a concise lesson, urging caution against
relying too heavily on our efforts
accurately to capture and communicate
our thoughts.

«»

*"What you learn is that language is an
infinitely more devious and slippery medium
than you had supposed."*

David Lodge, Nice Work

This author gives us two explanations for why words may not obey our thoughts. The first uses personification to suggest that words have "minds of their own."

«»

*One cannot be too careful with words, they change their minds just as people do.*

José Saramago, *Death with Interruptions*

His second effort is more specific and more colorful, using metaphors that emphasize how words are ephemeral.

«»

*...words move, they change from one day to the next, they are as unstable as shadows, are themselves shadows, which both are and have ceased to be, soap bubbles, shells in which one can barely hear a whisper, mere tree stumps.*

José Saramago, *Death with Interruptions*

If the preceding difficulties were not causing enough trouble, we now find that words may take on all kinds of characteristics that may escape us.

«»

*There seemed to be some metric regulation to the pace of the talk. It was emotional, intimate, evocative and as random as poetry.*

John Cheever, *Bullet Park*

We may blame our "failure to communicate" (recall the famous line from the Paul Newman movie, Cool Hand Luke) on the tools at our disposal, but even if they were functional, we may not be capable of using them accurately and completely to convey our thoughts and feelings. We start with an equivocation, which does not offer any help.

«»

*Is it possible to describe anything accurately?… The answer is, like so many answers to important questions, neither yes or no.*

*Gore Vidal, Myra Breckenridge*

Even if we can muster the correct words
from our limited vocabulary, there
remains this question.

«»

*Can anyone effect change with words?*
      Carlos Fuentes, *The Eagle's Throne*

Was this character's problem that she had too much in her mind, a lack of adequate words, her inability to use the ones she had, or some combination of these?

«»

*Bea had a sense of needing every word at her disposal if she were ever to voice even half the best, often times peculiar, thoughts inside her.*

Brad Leithauser, *The Art Student's War*

Here is another allusion to the notion that the more we think and feel the less we may be able to convey our thoughts and feelings.

*On earth they would never discuss a thing. Silent impressions would have to do. Incommunicable diversities, kindly but silent contact. The more they had in their heads, the less people seemed to know how to tell it.*

Saul Bellow, "The Old System"
in *Mosby's Memoirs
and Other Stories*

16

Am I the only (or person) who starts talking before he knows precisely what he will be saying? By the way, I do not consider myself a "great talker."

«»

*Great talkers are so constituted that they do not know their own thoughts until, on the tide of their particular gift, they hear them issuing from their mouths.*

*Thornton Wilder, The Woman of Andros*

Here is another, very brief expression of a similar notion. Lawyers will often advise clients who are witnesses to think through what they will say before answering a question, but it is very much "easier said than done."

«»

*...but he thinks out loud. He still hasn't learned to rehearse what he'll say later.*

*Carlos Fuentes, The Eagle's Throne*

This seems to be an extreme case of an inability to express oneself adequately.

«»

*Most of life gives language the slip anyway, I find. Look at me: I rattle all day long and into the night and say only a fraction of what I feel, a fraction of what is in my heart.*

Dennis McFarland, Nostalgia

Here we have, at least or at last, some suggestion of how to deal with our lack of proper tools and our incapacities.

«»

*Discretion, oddly enough, is the best response for a man of stalled responses.*

Richard Ford, *The Sportswriter*

I like this one because it starts out with such a positive reaction to the speaker's abilities but ends with a sly bit of criticism.

《》

*Nobody she thought ever had even talked like him, or could possibly talk like him. His voice was so clear and bright, like the best sort of print. Only sometimes you wished you had spectacles.*

H. G. Wells, *Christina Alberta's Father*

I had not thought of this task as being so important, but having read this, I can think of times when I wish I had been better able to do it.

«»

*...changing the subject is one of the most difficult arts to master, the key to almost all others.*

*César Aira,* An Episode in the Life of a Landscape Painter

Is this universal? Even if it is not, it probably applies to people who love someone because loving someone often leads to some disappointment.

«»

*Why is it so hard to articulate love yet so easy to express disappointment?*

Kaui Hart Hemmings,
*The Descendants*

I cannot help but be amused by the metaphors used to compare poor communications in two seemingly remote contexts.

«»

*The level of communication in a madhouse... was not much different from that of a typical press conference, except that the questions [in the madhouse] seemed more intelligent.*

William Kotzwinkle, *The Exile*

Most everyone has a secret, but do we think about how strongly, if at all, we want it always to remain a secret?

«»

*...there will always come a moment when we must ask ourselves if the dream, the ambition, the secret hope of all secrets, is, in fact, the possibility, however vague, however remote, of ceasing to be a secret.*

José Saramago, *The Cave*

I like this reminder that words and our intentions in using them may not always be for the purpose of revealing our true thoughts and feelings.

«»

*The epigrammatic saying that speech has been given to us for the purpose of concealing our thoughts came to his mind.*

*Joseph Conrad*, Under Western Eyes

I like this quote because of its concise
expression of a human foible and
how it does so humorously.

«»

*Very few people will turn down a direct
invitation to talk about themselves....*

David Lodge, Home Truths

Here are a few quotes which remind us that much of our talk or speech has little or no meaningful content. This occurs not only in "cocktail party" conversation but also in communications with our close relations and our professional colleagues. I suspect we have all experienced how others have been guilty of this, but do we recognize instances in which we have spoken but conveyed little or nothing? The first uses a metaphor that will displease some who are avid card-players.

«»

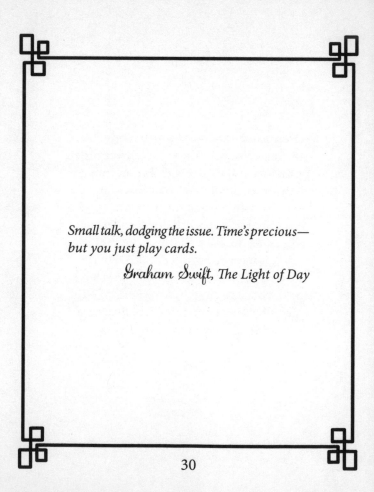

*Small talk, dodging the issue. Time's precious—*
*but you just play cards.*

Graham Swift, *The Light of Day*

The admonition to talk only when we
have something meaningful to say,
if taken literally, or to the extreme,
would have profound consequences,
as imagined here.

«»

*But if nobody spoke unless he had something
to say...the human race would very soon
lose the use of speech.*

W. Somerset Maugham,
*The Painted Veil*

I would wager that most of us have found ourselves in circumstances like these.

«»

*This was one of the occasions where much was spoken, but very little was actually being said.*

Ivan Doig, *The Bartender's Tale*

I suppose hearing the same stories, like some of the ones I tell, can seem a lot like a lack of meaningful content.

《》

*So little remains the same in this life that one can only take pleasure in a man who persists in telling you, year after year, the same stores in precisely the same words.*

Gore Vidal, Creation

The "flipside," if you will, to the quotes
on the preceding topic is lots of quantity,
with or without content, but so excessive
that the effort is in vain. What causes
some people to drone on, perhaps,
a lack of adequate listeners? Again,
I am sure most readers will have been
on the receiving end, but how often
are we on the offering end?

«»

*He has a good voice, but like most people
with a good voices or ideas that they
consider good, he finds it hard to stop.*

John Hersey, *The Conspiracy*

I suspect most of us talk mainly to people we know, and only occasionally talk with or to people we do not know.

«»

*If you started talking to strangers, where would it stop?*

John Lanchester, Mr. Phillips

Some of us may have had to learn through
experience that less can be more.

«‹›»

*People tended to be very spendthrift with
their language...they used a lot more words
than they needed to.*

Anne Tyler, *Vinegar Girl*

Here are two related observations about
a character who does a lot more than
overdo it.

«»

*...his perpetual and endless monologue
has one virtue: It has the power to turn
practically any audience catatonic....*

*...his speeches are so boring that he doesn't
just put his audience to sleep, he puts himself
to sleep, too!*

*Carlos Fuentes, The Eagle's Throne*

This quote "rings a bell" for me because there were times after graduation from high school when it seemed like many of my old friends wanted to tell and retell the same stories of some of our highs and lows together.

«»

*You can't keep on talking forever about what a hell of a good time you had when you were kids.*

Robert Penn Warren,
*All the King's Men*

From one of my favorite authors comes a very concise and ironic expression of one of the effects of excessive talking.

«»

*She was a nonstop talker, which made her hard to know....*

Kurt Vonnegut, Jr., *Mother Night*

# Negative and Positive Effects

Regardless of whether or not our failures to communicate effectively are caused by words alone, our inabilities or both, our efforts are sometimes not only ineffective but also counterproductive. Don't you hate that? Sometimes we do not try hard enough and do not think in advance about the potential effects of what we are going to say. Other times we do not know our audience so well as we think we do.

We may not intend to inflict any harm, but we occasionally do, either through carelessness or lack of appreciation for how our words will affect others.

«»

*D'you know what happens when you hurt people?...When you hurt people, they begin to love you less. That's what careless words do. They make people love you a little less.*

Arundhati Roy, *The God of Small Things*

This quote makes our communication efforts sound like a game of chance, with the odds stacked against us.

«»

*He saw that everything you say says either more than you wanted it to say or less than you wanted it to say; and everything you do does either more than you wanted it to do or less than you wanted it to do. What you said and did made a difference all right, but not the difference you intended.*

*Philip Roth*, American Pastoral

Does this mean we should give up?  The
main character is this novel is obsessed
with independence, does not want to be
influenced or persuaded by others and has
no interest in persuading others.

«»

*...it is a mark of weakness to try to talk
anyone over.*

*Halldor Laxness, Independent
People*

45

Here is a quote that reminds us that
we may not know our audience so
well as we should.

«»

*No one enjoys being reminded of all that he
has not accomplished in his life.*

Gore Vidal, *Creation*

For a playwright known for his wit and
humor, this character offers a very
serious admonition.

《》

*Actions are the first tragedy in life. Words
are the second. Words are perhaps the
worst. Words are merciless....*

Oscar Wilde, Lady Windemere's
Fan

Ok, so sometimes, whether in haste or a pique, we say something that we regret, but even to those we love?

«»

*"Few can resist the pleasure of saying something disagreeable, even to their nearest and dearest."*

Louis Auchincloss, "The Lotos Eaters," in *Tales of Yesteryear*

It is a bit discouraging to understand
that we often do not understand how our
words will be taken, even by people we
think we know well and who, at least,
seem to know us well.

«»

*Some talk has an obvious meaning
and nothing more...and some, often
unbeknownst to the talker, has at least one
other meaning and sometimes several other
meanings lurking around inside its obvious
meaning.*

Joseph Mitchell, "Joe Gould's Secret"
in *Up in the Old Hotel*

Other complications are our conflicting thoughts and emotions that confuse our communications.

«»

*...words often have very different effects from those intended, so much that these men and women quite often curse and swear, I hate her, I hate him, then burst into tears when they've done so.*

José Saramago, *Death with Interruptions*

I tell lots of stories, usually in complete confidence that I know what they will mean to people who hear them. I guess I should be more careful.

«»

*Yeah, but none of our stories mean what we think they do.*

Richard Russo, "Milton and Marcus" in *Trajectory*

Here is a quote for the superstitious among us. Yet even when our rationality governs, we may be loath to name our fears lest the feared thing will come true as a result of speaking of it. Being able to say "I told you so" is usually not sufficient consolation.

«»

*She believed that by giving problems a name they tended to manifest themselves, and then it was impossible to ignore them; whereas, if they remained in the limbo of unspoken words, they could disappear by themselves, with the passage of time.*

Isabel Allende, *The House of Spirits*

Now, we get to enjoy reading about some of the positive effects of our efforts to communicate. Some of the effects are for our own benefit, while others benefit our audience, and some may do both.

«»

*There was nothing nicer, he thought, than speaking when you really had something to say, when you had the power to affect with mere words the body chemistry of your listener....*

David Carkeet, Double Negative

Do we not enjoy it when our words offer solace to the hearer?

«»

*Good words are a vain benevolence that demands no sacrifice and is more appreciated than real acts of kindness.*

*Carlos Ruiz Zafón, The Angel's Game*

Not everyone may feel this enthusiasm,
but I know I do like to share some of
my experiences, adventures and
lessons learned.

«»

*...telling about things is one of the joys of
life.*

*Primo Levi*, The Monkey Wrench

The main character in this novel extolls
the virtues of talk, something the author
allows many of this characters to do.
Perhaps, the feeling may be mutual
between the speaker and his or
her audience.

«›»

*...I like to talk. It is the only civilized thing
we have. How otherwise can we divert
ourselves?*

*Ernest Hemingway*, For Whom
the Bell Tolls

The character here is describing how he came to have a different view of his wife, albeit with a result that led to the end of the marriage. Win some; lose some.

«»

*But she could talk, and when something talks you sooner or later begin to listen to the sound it makes and begin, even in the face of all the other evidence, to regard it as a person.*

Robert Penn Warren,
*All the King's Men*

Reading this made me realize how true it can be. At least someone's use of the tactic might make me likely to disclose the secret.

«»

*It's true enough; there's no surer way of getting a secret than by letting on you know it already.*

George MacDonald Fraser,
*Flashman and the Tiger*

We should conclude this section with a profound exposition of how valuable our efforts may be.

«»

*When we strike up a conversation, we are often trying to work out what our interlocutor is thinking. And it seems impossible to ascertain those thoughts except by a long series of inferences. What could be more closed off and mediated than someone else's mental activity? And yet this activity is expressed in language, words resounding in the air, simply waiting to be heard. We come up against words, and before we know it, we are already emerging on the other side, grappling with the thought of another mind.*

César Aira, *An Episode in the Life of a Landscape Painter*

# Lies, Liars, and Truth

It may come as no surprise to readers that authors and their characters describe a great deal of mendacity and explore the consequences of it for everyone. There are all sorts of falsehoods, such as, the little "white" lies that we tell in an effort not to harm someone. Then there are the untruths that we use to mislead others. The effects on the person or people lied to seem obvious, but worth exploring.

I hope the first part of this quote is an exaggeration but acknowledge the likelihood of the second part.

«»

*Everyone lied. Lies were at everyone's disposal, waiting to be picked up when there was a use to put them to.*

William Trevor, "A Perfect Relationship" in *Cheating at Canasta*

It seems unfair to pick upon this
profession. I am sure all of us can
think of others that might deserve this
criticism. My former profession was the
object of many jokes that implied general
dishonesty among its practitioners.

«»

*They say he lies more than a dentist....*

*Carlos Fuentes, The Eagle's Throne*

65

From the same novel comes an admonition about the effort lying takes, along with an identification of a profession that is renowned for liars and lying.

《》

"That lying successfully requires an enormous amount of time attention. The successful cultivation of lie is a full-time job. Which is precisely what political life allows for."

Carlos Fuentes, *The Eagle's Throne*

I like the focus on the effects of a lie upon the liar, a consequence that one might miss when he or she considers lying.

«»

*He was unused to the awful compression that comes with a lie, when it dawns upon the liar that the lie he has uttered is one to which he is now bound; that he must now keep lying, and compound smaller lies upon the first, and be shuttered in lonely contemplation of his own mistake.*

Eleanor Catton, The Luminaries

It may be obvious, but if one intends to mislead others, he or she may or may not succeed, but failure to deceive may have unforeseen consequences.

«»

*But the lie had to a good one, because if your lie is badly done it makes everyone feel wretched, liar and lied-to alike plunged into the deepest lackadaisy....*

Donald Barthelme, "And Then" in *Amateurs*

So, if we cannot lie well, we should not bother and just stick with the truth.

«»

*There are men who fib with so bad a grace and with so little tact that they might as well not fib at all.*

Anthony Trollope, The Claverings

I like the "it takes one to know one"
element in this quote, taken just a
step further.

«»

*Nobody can feel more compassion for a*
*fibber than another fibber.*

*Carlos Ruiz Zafon, The Shadow of*
*the Wind*

The following quotes offer some insightful observations upon the relationships between lies and truth. I do not agree with the first part of the first quote; the second part must be an exaggeration, but it is a worthwhile one.

«»

*"There are few reasons for telling the truth, but for lying the number is infinite."*

Carlos Ruiz Zafón, *The Shadow of the Wind*

This quote makes us consider two issues. Can we discern lies from the truth? If we stray from the truth, are we able to do so without detection?

《》

*He knew that; everyone told lies. It was for the intelligent man to distinguish truth from lies, just as it was only the intelligent man who knew how to lie in a way that made it next to impossible for others to find his lies and identify them as such.*

Paul Bowles, *The Spider's House*

I am very fond of this quote, and it makes me ask the same question about email and text messages. Technology can help us communicate but can also lead to misunderstandings or worse.

«»

*...you can't tell the truth on the telephone.*
T. S. Eliot, *"The Cocktail Party"*

It would be comforting if it were all as
simple and just as this.

«◊»

*A liar falls sooner than a one-legged man.*

*Carlos Fuentes*, The Eagle's Throne

I felt tired after reading the quote below; it seems like such a conundrum between lies and truth and our ability in a timely manner to determine which is which.

《》

*...there are many lies and no truths, well, there must be some out there, but they are continually changing, and not only does a possible truth give us insufficient time to consider its merits, we also have to check first that this possible truth is not, in fact, a probable lie.*

José Saramago, The Cave

I especially like the combined wit and wisdom of this character's observation. There is some truth to it, is there not?

«»

*...I have yet to come across a really inspired liar who was not positively lyric on the virtue of truth-telling.*

Gore Vidal, Creation

Here is a consideration to remember for
its perspicacity of the analysis
and conclusion.

«»

*He reasoned as follows: in principle, telling
the truth and lying require the same amount
of effort, so why not tell the truth, without
omissions or ambiguities?*

César Aira, An Episode in the Life
of a Landscape Painter

So, now we may be back to the problem of language with an aspiration for a theoretical solution.

《》

*There ought to be a whole separate language, she thought, for words that are truer than other words—for perfect, absolute truth.*

*Anne Tyler, Dinner at the Homesick Restaurant*

# Silence and Other Means of Communication

We may not usually think of silence as a part of communication, but it is an important one. Think of the times you have found a person's silence to be full of meaning. Have you used silence to convey your feelings in response to someone's assertions or questions? Sometimes, it may be, as suggested below, to be the best alternative. Depending upon the context silence may have a positive or negative effect. We often use the phrase, "silence is golden," but we may not be sure what it means when we meet it. It might signal thoughtfulness before speaking or a lack of something cogent to say. It might also be a very calculated way to keep us talking more than we would otherwise want.

I appreciate the irony in this quote, but
wonder if it a bit of hyperbole.

«»

*There is nothing like a vow of silence to
loosen the tongue.*

*Gore Vidal*, Creation

The narrator in this story extolls the virtues of information as a source of power but very briefly cites another one.

«»

*...silence, too, can be power.*

Carlos Fuentes, "The Prisoner of Las Lomas" in *Constancia and Other Stories for Virgins*

I wonder if intentionality or lack thereof makes a difference. How can we tell if another's silence is intentional or not?

«»

*Untended silence was anarchy, potentially anyone's, an unacceptable free-for-all.*

Robert Stone, *Outerbridge Reach*

From the listener's perspective deception
is unwelcome when it is discovered.
What may be worse is when the listener
perceives there is something to be learned
but cannot discern it because of the lack
of speech.

«»

*...many of the words he uttered were merely*
*smoke screens, which, in a way, is hardly*
*surprising, since words are often used for*
*precisely that purpose, but it's worse still*
*when the words remain unspoken and*
*become a thick wall of silence, because,*
*when confronted by such a wall, it's hard to*
*know what to do....*

José Saramago, *The Cave*

I think these exaggerated condemnations
must be the result of numerous bad
experiences.

«»

*Being mute is a form of nagging. Silence is
aggressive.*

Paul Theroux, Hotel Honolulu

Aggressive is one thing, but is it true
that we speak to some silent people
at your peril?

«»

*Wordless people can be dangerous, for no
other reason than they are wordless. Chatter
to them and they are provoked.*

Paul Theroux, *Hotel Honolulu*

I like the very concise example of how silence can be better than saying something, at least for some people.

«〉»

*Silence makes even idiots seem wise for a minute.*

Carlos Ruiz Zafon, *The Angel's Game*

Good lawyers learn that there are times to remain silent, not just when arrested, but also in arguments and negotiations.

«»

*Fallon said nothing. Sometimes it was the best thing to say.*

William Martin, Harvard Yard

If some restraint is a good thing, maybe more is even better.

«»

*...the mouth is an organ that is all the more trustworthy the more silent it is.*

José Saramago, *The Cave*

I wish I were better at using silence, especially tamping down my eagerness to reply and "chime in."

«»

*For most of us, it is the silences which express feeling, and perhaps inhibit it.*

Gore Vidal, *Two Sisters*

The idea that we communicate through means other than spoken words is not surprising. Think of "body language," for example. Written words can be more meaningful and longer lasting than talk. As with oral communications, alternatives can accomplish more, less or something different from what we intend. I find the first quote very creative.

«»

*In a lonely fantasy of nomadism he imagined a world where men and women communicated with one another mostly by signal lights [on cars] and where he proposed marriage to some stranger because she turned on her parking lights an hour before dusk, disclosing a supple and romantic nature.*

John Cheever, *Oh What a Paradise It Seems*

If understanding another person's words can be difficult, just imagine how hard it may be to decode another person's facial expressions.

«»

*One thing you learned was that reading peoples' faces was an extremely dubious pastime.*

Wallace Stegner, Second Growth

Facial expressions can, however, communicate a great deal, effectively and efficiently sending all sorts of messages.

«»

*But he had a smile on his face like he didn't expect for one moment to be blamed for anything. It was the way one apologized when they'd tried to do you a favor, but it hadn't worked out.*

Kazuo Ishiguro, Never Let Me Go

The princess, the hostess at the dinner party, had ways of communicating with just her looks that seemed very effective.

《》

*[She] gave him another of those quiet smiling looks of hers-in which there was the indulgence of an old rip who has neither forgotten nor repented of her naughty past and at the same time the shrewdness of a woman who knows the world like the palm of her hand and come to the conclusion that no one is any better than he should be.*

W. Somerset Maugham,
*Up At The Villa*

I am glad I found this quote, even though the observation seems pretty obvious, that is, many of us dress "for the occasion," that is, for our professional roles and recreational endeavors, with more or less care.

«»

*[She] was well aware that clothes do not merely serve the practical purpose of covering our bodies, but also convey messages about who we are, what we are doing, and how we feel.*

David Lodge, *Nice Work*

From the same novel, a principal character describes why telephone conversation is a murky middle ground. The idea is related to the quote from T. S. Eliot.

«»

*The telephone is an unsatisfactory medium for communicating anything important, allowing neither the genuine absence of writing nor the true presence of face-to-face conversation, but only a feeble compromise.*

David Lodge, *Nice Work*

*The word that is written is a thing capable of permanent life, and lives frequently to the confusion of its parent. A man should make his confessions always by word of mouth if it be possible.*

Anthony Trollope, The Claverings

# Listening and Audience

Some of us may have learned the hard way how important listening is. In my negotiations for business transactions, I learned that often listening and waiting before responding can be very valuable. One negotiator explained how he would interpret his side's proposal while his colleagues cringed because he was making my counterarguments more effectively than I could have done. In personal relations, I have found listening to be much appreciated.

I hope I am not the only one who is often thinking what I am going to say while the other person is talking.

«»

*...(he has the ability to listen while talking—a rare gift, alas, not mine).*

Gore Vidal, *Two Sisters*

This cannot be overstated for married men; wives often do not want a proposed solution to their problems and would be happier just knowing they are being heard.

«»

*Listening is good, he thought, listening is always good.*

*Martin Amis, The Information*

I like the comparison of listening to telling and agree I do not know where to find the instruction manual.

《》

*...just as there is an art of story-telling, strictly codified through thousands of trials and errors, so there is an art of listening, equally ancient and noble, but as far as I know, it has never been given any norm.*

Primo Levi, *The Monkey Wrench*

Having been a law firm lawyer whose time was billed to clients and a factor in compensation decisions, I appreciate the simile here. (Please note that the current standard is in tenths of an hour.)

«»

*As soon as I began speaking she got impatient, as though I were wasting her time and she had more important things to do, like the lawyer in whose eyes you see thoughts of billable hours, and who, even at his idlest, becomes a clock watcher in conversation, talking in quarter-hour increments.*

Paul Theroux, *Hotel Honolulu*

A very valuable principle for effective communication is to "know your audience." Some audiences are knowledgeable and sophisticated, but no matter how much so, we may be misunderstood. We may overestimate our audience's ability to absorb or accept our words. I will never forget the realization as a very junior lawyer that clients seemed to be accepting and acting on my advice.

《》

*Sometimes it was hard to say things. Things were so complicated. People might resent what you said. They might use your remarks against you. They might be indifferent to your remarks. They might take you seriously and act upon your words, actually do something. They might not even hear you, which perhaps was the only thing worth hoping for. But it was more complicated than that. The sheer effort of speaking. Easier to stay apart, leave things as they are, avoid responsibility for reflecting the world and all its grave weight. Things that should be simple are always hard. But hard things are never easy.*

Don Delillo, *Ratner's Star*

It is perhaps no surprise that this author offers us a rather pessimistic outlook on the prospects of being understood.

«»

*Most of us continue under the ready assumption that we are being understood, and that we understand others, forgetting that the human level of attention isn't very reliable.*

*Jim Harrison,* Dalva

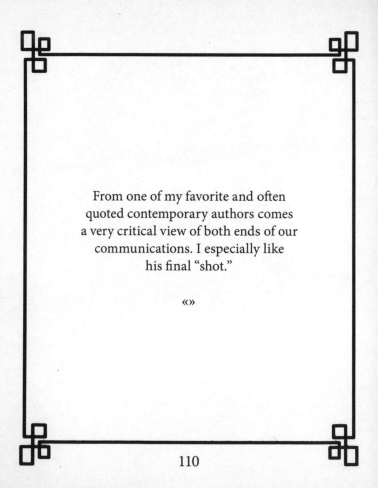

From one of my favorite and often
quoted contemporary authors comes
a very critical view of both ends of our
communications. I especially like
his final "shot."

«»

We humans are winging it, improvising. Input pattern *x* sets off associative matrix *y*, which bears only the slightest relevance to the stimulus and is often worthless. Conscious intelligence is smoke and mirrors. Almost free-associative. Nobody really responds to anyone else, per se. We all spout our canned and thumb-nailed scripts, with the barest minimum of polite segues. Granted, we're remarkably fast at indexing and retrieval. But comprehension and appropriate response are often more on the order of buckshot.

*Richard Powers, Galatea 2.2*

For readers who are parents, the quote below may resonate, even if it is a bit of an exaggeration.

«»

*Embarrassment seems to be the sole means of communication between parents and children.*

Heinrich Böll, The Clown

I have always been in favor of using some humor in my negotiations and teaching, but I may have had less appreciation for humor interjected by my audience.

«»

*Anyway, humor for a monologuist is an unwelcome interruption.*

Paul Theroux, *Hotel Honolulu*

Here is a description of an undesirable, to say the least, audience. Wow!

«»

"...talking to you is like finding oneself in a labyrinth with no doors, Now that's an excellent definition of life..."

José Saramago, *Death with Interruptions*

This character makes a reasonable
observation, but the question at the end
may be rhetorical.

«»

*...sometimes one feels freer speaking to a
stranger than to people one knows. Why is
that?*

*Carlos Ruiz Zafon*, The Shadow of
the Wind

It seems pretty easy to agree with the part of this quote regarding someone who has learned something bad about himself or herself, but cannot we find something to say when it has been good?

«»

*There isn't ever anything to say to somebody who has found out the truth about himself, whether it is good or bad.*

Robert Penn Warren,
*All the King's Men*

The life-long, powerful politician in this novel may have become one of the worst possible audiences.

«»

*My eyes avert all attempts at conversation—whether they are friendly, unfriendly, unpleasant, sincere, ambiguous or impertinent conversations. For me, anything and everything people say represents a potential danger. The danger of contradiction in the best cases. The danger of persuasion in the worst.*

Carlos Fuentes, *The Eagle's Throne*

So, is the key to successful communications to have intercourse with only suitable audiences?

«»

*It made no difference how bleak the situation appeared to be. The apt phrase tended to settle matters. No action is more suitable than the apt phrase. Of course, one addresses such a phrase only to suitable people.*

Don Delillo, *Ratner's Star*

Do we have expectations of reciprocity,
and, if so, are they realistic?

《》

*The thing about confidences—the unsolicit-
ed opening of the heart—is that they invite
reciprocity, even when it's not a good idea....*

Richard Russo, "Milton and Marcus"
in *Trajectory*

As a former tennis player, I was not a great server and did not put lobs away very well. So much for the tennis metaphor for me.

《》

*Also, in that same tennis match, we serve confidences to people we hope will lob their own secrets back to us.*

Paul Theroux, *Hotel Honolulu*

How often are we ourselves our principal audience? It seems viable when we are by ourselves.

«»

*Nobody was around to hear him talking to himself, which was one of the best parts of being alone.*

Anthony Doerr, *All the Light We Cannot See*

Even if we are seemingly talking to
another person, our main audience may
be ourselves. I hope you appreciate the
author's humor as much as I do.

«»

*...but it often happens that talking some-
thing over with someone has the effect
of clarifying one's thoughts, even if that
someone merely gapes at one like a goldfish.*

P. G. Wodehouse, *A Pelican at
Blandings*

You will realize that I have saved this one
for last. The author should be no surprise.

«»

*"I speak gibberish to the civilized world,
and it replies in kind."*

Kurt Vonnegut, Jr., Mother Night

# That's all folks

Some of our conversations get off to a bad start. Others begin well but "go downhill" or "off the rails" gradually or quickly. Whether it is a dialogue or monologue, we (usually) want to be understood and receive some feedback to that effect. Sometimes, despite our best efforts, we fail, and at other times, we seem to succeed beyond our hopes and expectations. I hope that my effort here has been worth readers' attention—perhaps, thought-provoking, amusing or both. At least, it will not go on and on and on…

*I would like to express my deep appreciation for Tyson Cornell's enthusiastic support and creative ideas for this third volume of my quotations, and for the hard work by all of the staff at Rare Bird, including Alice Marsh-Elmer for the development and execution of the excellent design, inside and out, of the book; Hailie Johnson; Julia Callahan; Guy Intoci; and Jessica Szuszka.*

*Thanks to Cara Lowe for the illustrations.*

*...all luck, dodging the issue. Time runs short—*
*but you just play cards.*

*Graham Swift, The Light of Day*